The story of the good Samaritan

Story by Penny Frank
Illustrated by Tony Morris

THE LION
STORY BIBLE

38

TRING · BATAVIA · SYDNEY

The Bible tells us how God sent his Son Jesus to show us what God is like and how we can belong to God's kingdom.

This is a story Jesus told to show that God wants everyone in his kingdom to be ready to help others.

You can find this story in your own Bible in Luke's Gospel, chapter 10.

Copyright © 1985 Lion Publishing

Published by
Lion Publishing plc
Icknield Way, Tring, Herts, England
ISBN 0 85648 763 5
Lion Publishing Corporation
1705 Hubbard Avenue, Batavia,
Illinois 60510, USA
ISBN 0 85648 763 5
Albatross Books Pty Ltd
PO Box 320, Sutherland, NSW 2232, Australia
ISBN 0 86760 548 0

First edition 1985
Reprinted 1986

Printed and bound in Hong Kong

British Library Cataloguing in Publication Data

Frank, Penny
   The story of the good Samaritan. –
(The Lion Story Bible; 38)
   1. Good Samaritan *(Parable)* –
Juvenile literature
I. Title
226'.809505   BT.378.G6

ISBN 0-85648-763-5

Library of Congress Cataloging in Publication Data

Frank, Penny.
The story of the good Samaritan.
(The Lion Story Bible; 38)
1. Good Samaritan (Parable)—Juvenile
literature. [1. Good Samaritan
(Parable) 2. Parables. 3. Bible
stories—N.T.] I. Morris, Tony, ill.
II. Title. III. Series: Frank, Penny.
Lion Story Bible; 38.
BT378.G6F7 1985   226'.409505
84-25023
ISBN 0-85648-763-5

Among the people who came to hear
Jesus there were always some who tried
to make him look silly in front of the
crowds.

They thought up trick questions to ask
him because they were jealous of the
way all the people listened to him.

One day a teacher of God's Law came up to Jesus and asked a question.

'I want to have the eternal life you talk about,' he said. 'What must I do?'

Jesus answered, 'What does God's Law tell you to do?'

'It tells me to love God with all my heart
and mind, and to love other people as I
love myself.'

'That's right,' Jesus said. 'So what
don't you understand?'

The teacher had tried to trick Jesus with his question. But Jesus was too clever.

He thought quickly. 'But what does that mean?' he asked.

'Listen to this story,' said Jesus, 'and you will know the answer.'

7

All the crowd listened quietly while Jesus told the story.

'There was a man, all on his own, going down the dangerous road from Jerusalem to Jericho.

'Suddenly some robbers jumped out from
behind the rocks at the side of the road.
They beat him up and took all his
money. Then they ran away.

'The road wasn't busy and it was quite a while before anyone came by.

'The first man who came was a priest. He was a bit frightened when he saw that there was a body at the side of the road.

'He was scared in case the men came back and attacked him. So he hurried by, on the other side of the road.

'The next person to come along was a Levite, who helped to look after God's temple in Jerusalem.

'He crossed the road to have a look, but he couldn't decide if the man was dead or alive. So he hurried on.'

The crowd nodded. They knew no one could go into God's temple after touching a dead body.

'The next person coming down the road was a Samaritan.'

The crowd began to look uncomfortable. Jews hated Samaritans. What would happen next?

Jesus went on: 'The Samaritan got off his donkey when he saw the man. He took water and some soft cloth from his saddlebags.

'He saw that the man was still alive. The Samaritan cleaned the man's cuts and bruises and gave him a drink.

'When he had bandaged him up, the Samaritan lifted the man onto his donkey. He led the donkey gently down the road until they reached the inn.

'The Samaritan often stayed at that inn. The innkeeper knew him well. Soon the hurt man was safe and comfortable.

'The next day, the Samaritan had to
continue his journey, but first he spoke
to the man who owned the inn, and
gave him some money.

' "I want you to keep on looking after
the man who was hurt," he said. "Give
him good food and let him rest here
until he is well. If it costs you more than
I have given you, I will pay when I
come back." '

Jesus turned to the clever teacher of God's Law.

'Can you tell me which of those men really loved the man who was hurt?' he asked.

The teacher hated even to say the word
'Samaritan'.

'The one who took care of him,' he
muttered.

'That's the right answer,' said Jesus. 'The Samaritan saw someone in need and helped him.

'That's what you must do, if you want to have eternal life and belong to God's kingdom.'

The Lion Story Bible is made up of 52 individual stories for young readers, building up an understanding of the Bible as one story — God's story — a story for all time and all people.

The New Testament section (numbers 31–52) covers the life and teaching of God's Son, Jesus. The stories are about the people he met, what he did and what he said. Almost all we know about the life of Jesus is recorded in the four Gospels — Matthew, Mark, Luke and John. The word gospel means 'good news'.
   The last four stories in this section are about the first Christians, who started to tell others the 'good news', as Jesus had commanded them — a story which continues today all over the world.

The story of the Good Samaritan comes from the New Testament, Luke's Gospel, chapter 10. It is one of Jesus' best-known stories. Knowing that the teacher of the Law was trying to catch him out, Jesus made him answer his own question, from the Old Testament scriptures. The first commandment is to love God; the second is to treat our fellow human beings as we would want to be treated ourselves. If we were able to obey these commands we would receive eternal life. But the story shows how hard it is to love our enemies. We cannot gain eternal life by keeping God's commands: we are not good enough. Jesus' answer showed the man how much he needed the good news Jesus came to bring — that we can find eternal life through him.
   The next story in the series, number 39: *The story of the sower*, shows the different ways in which people respond when they hear the good news.